RUBBLE SQUARE

poems by

Adam Tavel

STEPHEN F. AUSTIN STATE UNIVERSITY PRESS 2022

Managing Editor: Kimberly Verhines
Book design: Katt Noble
Cover Art: "Hilma's Botany of Desire" by Madara Mason

ISBN: 978-1-62288-937-2

For more information:
Stephen F. Austin State University Press
P.O. Box 13007 SFA Station
Nacogdoches, Texas 75962
sfapress@sfasu.edu
www.sfasu.edu/sfapress

Distributed by Texas A&M Consortium
www.tamupress.com

for Stacy & George

Show me an angel and I'll paint one.
- Gustave Courbet

CONTENTS

I.

II.

III.

Watching Outtakes of Orson Welles Playing Othello on YouTube
1952

Resingeing his right palm each take,
Welles smothers candles out and raves
unblinking from the shadows that
he makes. Fair Desdemona quakes

atop their marriage bed behind
the lens, our only eye, and so
he stares beyond us like a scout
who's sprinted dazed to tell us how

our village burned. His collared fur,
a shameless opulence, is puffed
to hide the color of his neck.
He stole it from another set.

This face he wears, his own, not black
but poorly bronzed, is another theft
that bends all suffering around
his tongue. His left hand shields the wax

that's melted down into itself
and pooled so low two fingers mask
its wick. How easily he snuffs
it out and calls his wife a whore.

How easily his frantic baritone
unfurls its lines, as if they burned
right from his head, a living candle
that disappears to bear its light.

Jeremiah Johnson Starring Robert Redford

He drags his grief like a mailsack
across the slow stares of bison. They share
the forfeitures of winter. Each step stabs
a small throat in snow. From time to time
braves we're meant to hate leap
with bone-handled daggers, having slunk
riverbanks and cliffs. The story smothers
their namelessness. Jeremiah is a beard
growing longer, crystalized with ice.
Alone he eats his jerky, hunching
over a pink carnation of fire.
How easy it seemed, an hour
earlier, when his Flathead bride Swan
lay naked in furs and opened
herself, a lost country, jeweled
in starlight. She called him Johnson
because it was easier to say, because
when he spoke all she heard was wagons.
He resents her, he loves her, she dies
when another tribe finds her humming
in a cabin. We leave his proud scar
crossing snow-streaked mountains,
his loaded rifle bobbing horseback.
The credits rise with sad guitars.

Word Problem

for Diane Glancy

One hundred eighty thousand bison skulls
are stacked into a mountain featured here,
the caption reads, or so some archivists
approximate—an educated shrug.
This faded photo from 1870

blurs everywhere except the ghostly horns,
and they are blank as photocopied tests
a substitute hands out, each desk a sigh
she cannot name. If prayer-dance returned
the herd, if we peered resurrected furs

from our lookout on a cliff, would we count
migration's steaming snouts across the snow
and mark the mothers from their calves that strayed
behind in search of clumps of onion grass?
Or would sunset rifles smear the ice

so red again we'd drop down to our knees
so not to slip, butchering by starlight,
contented as the dapper merchant perched
atop the pile, assured his grin is profit?
The caption states the best market price

a ton of skulls might fetch was fifteen bucks.
Most shipped to China where they were ground
for fertilizer, though some were fashioned
into cups. Teacher, I have a bellyache.
Collect my test. You'll see I've left it blank.

Zooming the Pledge
for Graham

Through yawns our mousy mumblers begin
on beat but lose it at *allegiance*. The rest
is sibilance—a rush of groggy speech
that scratches at the ear, like travelers
on a foreign business flight delayed
who hiss at tarmac lights. Fidgety, they stand
so we can spot their favorite characters
on fleece pajama pants. Forty girls and boys,
two homerooms combined, stare blankly back
at faces in an advent calendar
where each opened square is blurred. Some hands
cross hearts, some tap chins or worm in hair.
Like scolded elves they fight the urge to laugh
when dogs go wagging past or someone farts.
The rushers get to *all* while some are stalled
on *God*. How many tongues trip up and fall
at *indivisible*? It's nearly over now.
Half awake and puffy-faced, both teachers scowl
to make them love a country they can't spell.

Before Photography

It was impossible to keep a face
by amber candlelight and fight the ache
named midnight, starless, sooty as the veil
graveyard gloves draped across a vanity
for good. Each time the widow closed her eyes
she saw less nose, less neck, less collar stains
dark as dimes spilling from a burned mite box.
When a daughter grew old enough to ask
what father looked like, she was told he was
this tall, the mantle held his pipe and hat,
your brothers hemmed his overalls. Sometimes
after a house was snores, one lonely hand
slid under sheets and found some pleasure there
remembering a silhouette of fog.

May Night
Willard Leroy Metcalf, 1906

The marble mansion glows, a butchered tusk.
Its grand estate is wild and wooded still
though grass that meets the portico is cut
so low it looks like moss, wearing arrowheads
of leaves in patchy dappled shade. The only light

besides the jaundiced sheen from stars is orange
and spilling from a window lamp, obscured
by prickly shrubs too tall to trim without
laddered shears. The orange is meant to draw
us from ourselves, like a diary in flame

or blood a mouth has spit across hot sand.
A patient eye may follow it to find
the maiden strolling robed in aimlessness,
a wan and regal specter, who trails
her nightgown like a tree-torn parachute.

Some yards away, she stares beyond the stairs
she left, their massive column pairs, the door
we cannot see. Alone and turned from us
her beauty is the beauty of a conch
half-glimpsed by lovers strolling down a strand

who think the world a storeroom full of props,
who stop to point and coo while holding hands
then watch the surf return it to the sea.
Whose grumbles has she fled? What father, son,
or groom has driven her desperate for air?

Never mind. She is pacing back inside
to bear their growl again, but lingers here
in forever's frame, not quite returned
from owl-swoop shadow-fall, another bride
who drags her dewy hem and cannot hide.

Cut-Paper Work
Anna Maria Garthwaite, 1707

Her scalpel shaped the property
exact, one lord's grand estate
in miniature: the mansion flanked
by fruit trees, two lions reared
atop the fountain sparkling,
the weary horseman's dashed return,
his carriage racing dark. The sprawl
of serfs, so dutiful and thin,
pack every space with hunts,
a good excuse Garthwaite found
to shape exquisite panicked deer
who leap forever from the bows
that aim at their escape. Such hands
at seventeen sufficiently
amazed her father, a clergyman,
to let her keep her art. Perhaps
it was the blossomed apple trees,
their branching tendrils delicate
as hair that earned his cold consent
between his sermonizing, the way
the pruner's ladder disappears
in bloom. Beyond, the ballyhoo
of dogs nip at stags. One bites
the leg of one who dies when we
imagine it. The only doe,
behind a sprawling herd, lags back
but isn't chased. She's sprinting hard,
back bent, not knowing that beyond
one fence she'll find another fence.

Child in Memphis
Dorothea Lange, 1938

The shack porch laced
with bean vines wears
the blaze of June.
This black and white
America
is knotted string
a mother's hands
have tied across
the absence of
a rail, from boards
to roof, so shoots
can trellis on
the air. The girl
who squints into
the whitened glare
behind the white
photographer
must know her door
hangs open for
the flies, mule dust,
and present tense
of sharecropping.
Maybe she dreams
the sound it makes,
a camera smashed
to glimmered shards
beneath her heels.
She's nine or ten.
Her limbs too lean
from overwork,
her knotted hands
rest on her smock.
Or so I guess.
I cannot know
them there, those wrists
that taper to
small knuckles clenched,
obscured by blooms.

Her Whispering Offstage Before She Read

This intro's shit. Before they drag me out
to gossip over pasta why don't we
drain my flask? That's right, you can't. I can't
believe so many lonely people flock
to readings here on Friday nights. Who picks
these times? One time (I may have told you this)
some lady asked if I could sign a book
I already signed. She bought it used online
and never opened it. I signed it *fuck*
the internet. You should have seen her glow
and flitter to her Audi. I might need help
loading unsold books back in my trunk. They live
in rust on spite. Sit tight. This ancient blouse
still fits. It's time to murder all these clowns.

II

A Dark Pool

Laura Knight, c. 1908 - 1918

Her crimson dress, a bugled artery,
flares in the coastal breeze. Our figure stands
bold as a wayward milkmaid who fled
the dread we call betrothal. This is her rock,
worn smooth by tides that rise to crash its face
above the eddied pool we must presume
sends back her wavered form each time she stares
into the bobbing pink larghissimo
of jellyfish. Their tentacles fan out
beneath her sandy feet perched in a crook,
gull-like. How far away two husbands are
is measured by her calm. They've left Lamorna's bells
again, a painter and her sunlit muse,
to clamber slipping up the moss-furred cliffs.

Four Paintings by Cassatt

I.
The Pensive Reader, 1894

She doubts it all: the hackneyed lovelorn plot,
soliloquies the brooding stable lad
pontificates to straw, the tedium
of a judge's teenage daughter scheming
her lamp wick down. Our reader sighs, or so
I make her sigh. Her swooping ponytail
fades to auburn brushwork, nebulous
as the hair a jilted suicide unties
to leap so it can splay in mud beside the creek.

II.
Woman Standing, Holding a Fan, 1879

Her dress is muted green with russet flecks
like vines of trellised beans in late July.
Alone, we find the figure's outstretched arm
indulging in a twirl so quick and plain
it does not catch the nearing light that falls
across the chair smothering in lilac blooms.
Victorian, absurdly large, her fan's
perfect scallop arcs, leading to a face
for which a boy would kneel to dare a keyhole peek.

III.
Summertime, 1894

These rowboat drifters lazing on a pond
are sweatless in their heavy sleeves and gloves.
Their season is a floating dream absorbed
in mallards, two, whose rainbow waters lap
impasto orange on pink and violet swirls,
reflectionless. They cannot see their own
faces spectral, wavering in current,
these sisters who have rowed themselves until
the sun-stained sailors clanging by the pier are flecks.

IV.

The Child's Bath, 1893

Our common holiness was always this—
a toddler raven-haired who dips her feet
into a basin where the mischief dirt
from a summer dusk in meadows rambling
will bloom the water dark. Its steam is felt
not seen. The room is middle class mélange,
a floral clash, American. Here is our shrine
to reconcile an ancient faith restyled:
a common mother cradling her common child.

Marie-Thérèse Walter Mourns the Death of her Former Lover
Pablo Picasso

ago when I was beautiful the sun
would kiss the leathered muscles of my walk
till Paris bent its smirking genius down
to flash his practiced appetite and woo
my breasts my head unreal which lured the world
each time his canvas froze me snaking lithe
on sofas chairs a ghost invisible
was making love to me against my will
the vines outsized these symbols obvious
and strangling tame my belly's swollen rune
his wife the moon across the boulevard
but now forever night balloons his fame
O daughter made from yellow lust we hang
in frames so patrons clutch their coats and gasp

An Engraving of a Woman Entering an Abortion Clinic
Godefroy Engelmann, early 19th c.

the theme is shame :: a weary lapwing drooped
upon the stair, she's far enough along
her belly shows :: crimson shawl, a parasol,
she's stalled between her damages :: it stings,
this moment right before her secret knock
will creak the secret door to lead her down
an outlaw corridor of sighs :: she weeps
the attendant maudlin tears that always mar
inked archetypes :: let's kerchief them and lift
her chin :: let's call her dear Marie :: the day's
a gray we may endure :: I'll stuff her purse
with francs :: O sister wince and squeeze my hand ::
the drizzle fades :: Paris wakes at noon :: see how
each café awning drips its peridots

On Millet's *The Gleaners*
    1857

The swollen russet knuckles of their hands
are darker than the soil that dusts their hems.
They have no countenances, these peasant French,
reduced to three bonnets bowing. We're meant
to see them as our mothers grubbing wheat,
triangular, stooped in breezeless heat,
yet somehow still too dignified for dung-
stained clogs. Idealized, these poor that hung
inside the Louvre repulsed those bourgeoisie
who pulled perfumed kerchiefs from their sleeves
to feign the painting's rustic stench might waft.
Perhaps they feared the thick-armed girls embossed
upon the harvest background most, whose lives
were brute, and biblical, and dashed by scythes.

The Pillory and the Steepled Dark
Joseph Wright's An Experiment on a Bird in the Air Pump, 1768

The suffocating cockatoo falls limp
inside a glass vacuum-bowl, its feathers
upturned and splayed from breathless panicking.
Its broad breast grays in candlelight, like snow
beside a bonfire where ashes mist
and cloak its sheen. Why not call this science
in 1768, this crowded room
of villagers who left their creaky dens
to plod with invitations scribbled down
beyond the pillory and the steepled dark:
the widower who instantly regrets
he brought his dainty daughters to recoil,
a pair of lovers young enough to need
a ruse to meet, the despondent poet
staring at a skull submerged in ooze
and two apprentices, prim and dapper
who dutifully mark each second's tick?
The amateur philosopher stares out
disheveled and amazed, feeling finally
the derangement of a god, the awful dream
his machinery contains. His weary son
hoists the empty cage back to the ceiling,
tugging gingerly at a pulley rope
that squeaks till taut. A boy knows how this ends.
He's seen resurrections work their spell
until no flood of air can lift a wing.
There are no eager watchers then, behind
the paint-chipped barn, when a sacrifice
is heaped into a sacrificial grave
he opens with the moonlight on his spade.

A Wooden Rooster

His comb is rigid as the teardrop teeth
that rust a ten-speed's gears across the shop.
A small cursive V, his yawning beak
crows forever, soundlessly atop
the carving bench where splintered daffodils
in cobwebs fade and mold unpainted blooms.
An almost second face, his garish tail
puffs and grimaces, a vulture's brooding.
Grandfather, your rooster keeps your lair
supported by a single tapered leg
beside a model church that stinks of mouse-musk.
In shadows aproning this farm at dusk
I linger, willing tools back on their pegs,
a candle lit with sawdust in its hair.

Sheep Above Vermilion Lakes
Illingworth Kerr, 1982

nine rams :: like colonels in denial
nine rams :: kings of rainbow cliffs
nine rams :: extractions of Cezanne
nine rams :: brown as maple bark
nine rams :: piano benches in snow
nine rams :: the shape of their forgetting
nine rams :: a splintered wagon wheel
nine rams :: gleaming freight cars
nine rams :: blank hostages of frost

nine rams :: their own puffed parkas
nine rams :: eyebrows on a ridge
nine rams :: clouds under clouds
nine rams :: a fraying congregation
nine rams :: a liturgy of hunger
nine rams :: worn hermits grazing
nine rams :: beyond whose torn map
nine rams :: we have no trail out

Girl with Death Mask
Frida Kahlo, 1938

she's stripped the monster off to feel
cold hemispheres of bone
the limits of a landscape
where cyan mountains diminish
like knuckles in ligatures of snow

and the foreground indiscriminate
a patch as good as any to pretend
she has slipped inside unbeing
inside the blanched and common sheen
any grownup grave will bear

worn in mockery and praise
of faces we strain to recollect
at night awake behind our eyes
the ones we beckon to despite
our drowsed recessionals

here is the flickered votive
as pallbearers hum the nave
here is the dandelion
clutched in a girl's small fist
one brute remainder of the sun

Slaughterhouse Ruins at Aledo
Gertrude Abercrombie, 1937

The roof that hid their final agony
is gone—just cracked plaster walls,
a knoll's crude shed or naked barren stall
blanched like the wolf a desert keeps, its pet
of bone. Dull chrome, the depthless Texas sky
bleeds gray on gray, a stagehand's anywhere
for plays where someone bounds outside to stroll
into their doom and glides there on a song.
Before I gave up teaching speech a girl
sniffed through her A, regaling us with how
the stickers on most killing floors now wear
headphones to drown out bleats. She scowled
at our applause. Her gory posterboard,
a triptych altarpiece, got graded shut.
Small class. The stack was light. After exams
it flapped into the dumpster like a kite.

National Poetry Month

Alan, he kept calling me, Alan my medicine
is broke. He shook his empty flask
upside down, dour as a vicar. The rain

hammered my Silhouette as I shifted
into gear. No worries, I said, there's one
on every corner in this town. Selfishly

I hoped to hear about his prize, his ancient
love affairs—anything but eleven
bird poems on rumpled loose leaf,

mumbled on stage. The worst part of living
near the beach, he said, must be eventually
all your shirts smell like sunscreen.

Quaking, his left hand futzed with the dial
and found some Mahler. We drove and lost
the strings in static. An OPEN sign

flickered bloodshot. I tossed my wallet
in his lap. Behind the wave
of blades I watched him slosh into the light.

On a Photograph of Scott Weiland at the Virgin Festival, Calgary, 2008
   for Andrew Dewald

Mascara smear, megaphone, your Rolex glints
sundown at the lens. It's early in the set
because your shirt's still on, your loosened tie
a dangled crow beneath your scarf. This look

part glam, part corporate intern overtime
is seven years before your heart gives out
while wasted groupies wilt and clack their phones.
The weight you lost stays lost—so gaunt the press

declares each tour a relapse. How does it fray,
the patience for pretending to be saved
for kids, new wife, the band's back catalog?
Each city's shrieking girls swarm at your bus

and hold their baggies up beneath the glare
of loading docks behind the stadium.
Resist, we say, and shrug at songs that seem
mere remnants of our adolescent rage,

a dead decade, a movie we can't stand.
How many times are you in court until
you dress the same for gigs—a wry apology
for what we claim as ours, your body bent

into a note you still could hit? The mic
hangs at your side, a tuning interlude.
You're staring now beyond the dusk-drenched crowd,
those cloaked machines that fade the stage to smoke.

Phil Spector Points a Loaded Pistol

A bodyguard is reaching for the gun
that Spector levels at the camera lens.
It's 1975 forever here
inside a kitschy van, their arms thrust out
the trapezoid the driver's window left.
A stoned homunculus, his steel wool hair
combed up from sides across his scar-stitched scalp,
Spector dangles aviator shades
as nonchalantly as an oil tycoon
who learns mid-flight his third wife drowned on pills.
The sallow bearded goon's been up for days.
Stealthily he creeps his thumb to uncock
the hammer. We leave him petrified,
we distant targets past the barrel's aim.

Brutus's Feet

Jacques-Louis David's The Lictors Bring To Brutus
the Bodies of His Sons, 1789

David would have us praise the frigid stare
his Brutus fixes past the viewer's shock
into the manic gratitude he knows
the future holds. No matter that his wife
and daughters shriek to see these soldiers march
the stretcher-meat decapitated sons
now make, their lifeless marble legs
like limbs of broken kouroi in the ash
of the Acropolis, paler than the ankles
a father knots, annoyed with grief. The face
of Brutus says, women are girls who just
outgrew the cuteness of their stupidity.
Inside their wails he finds the fear he needs
to still his squirming heels. This republic
will last a thousand years or more, he thinks,
if we can find the courage to destroy
the tyranny of children with our blades.

Fury Grove

Henry Fuseli's Oedipus Cursing His Son, Polynices, 1786

Young Polynices crouches in the myth
that has him burn the name of Oedipus
from Theban lips and cast the cripple out,

a beggar king stumbling silver hills
bereft. When doomed rebellion sends
his shadow there to seek that father cursed

he finds just curse, a quavered arm, the growl
Apollo long ago gave to a prince
and let him keep, though servants later rinsed

mumbles from his beard. The moment Fuseli
demands we bear is masked and wordless cringe,
an ashen dusk where sisters hunch and grieve

the ragged thunder in their ears. Ismene,
her flame-hair frizzed, slumps like an arrowed fox.
Expressionless Antigone holds back

the father who, in one version of the tale,
she led beyond the city walls while gobs
of phlegm were hocked into her face.

Like prisoners they die and slap awake
to die again, roped to our broken chair,
chaffed wrists in knots. Inside this gilded frame

a father points across the dark and swears
both sons must die because their helpless flesh
is his, none more the dumbstruck penitent

his anxious hands once washed at birth and tried
to swaddle on midnight's sweat-drenched bed
where nurses cooed and scrubbed the blood away.

Cleaning the Colosseum
80 AD

It takes an hour for the merchant drunks
to filter out, our stragglers jangling coins
who spot their boyhood friends ten rows away
and bronze their brows in idle chitchat sweat,
avoiding their wives. What we overhear

is predictable and slurred: their Rome
clots with Gauls, their brothels sour more
each year, their second sons are sailing north
to freeze for mania. And then the flesh
below them, oozing, bakes to chase them out.

Our shadows pregnant with our sacks, we strain
like ants to clear the mangled bodies ripped
apart by roars. The smaller legs we save
for kennel whelps. You clever Decimus,
my master calls me jokingly, his favorite hands

because he sold ten daggers I snuck out
inside my belt. To think, I used to reel and retch
beside these maniacs and zealots split
like boars, the way their jutting ribs shone pink
against the moon. Now I make a game and guess

which leaking torso fought to save its god
and which for gold. Armless, the gray roots
of intestines spilled, I guess and drag
them into rows for younger slaves to heft.
Their sandals redden in my grove of chests.

A Man with a Cigarette
William Orpen, 1917

green ghost what's left to kill
so gaunt inside the trench
that France became: blue smear
of sky streaked white as if
the smoke from mortar rounds
could be your century's clouds:
the rest the earth your torn
fatigues are symphonies
of brown: Brodie helmet
rust-rimmed your eyeless face
shrunk withered as a prune:
the jacket where one arm
withdrawn inside balloons
so in its hidden sling
resembles pregnancy:
a joke too strained to work:
one pant leg tattered gone
is dangling there above
your bandaged calf that leads
the eye down to your boot
made laceless by the fight
to trudge half-deaf and starved:
here shivered wretch let's end
our dream of portraiture
with bones a limp the smoke
you hold inside your lungs
until it burns then swirls
and breaks against the cold
like steam that rises from
a boy who hugs his guts
and shrieks before he fails
to slop them back inside

Henri, Age 15, Amid the Verdun Siege
1916

Integer falcons, our lords of death ascend
as candidates of trees, the few not yet
undone. No statesmen here, they gloom what leaves
still cling to spite the ice. Who cast a vote
for them, for this, for canon-quakes? They shake
the plated bones that form my skull. I clutch
their shoddy stitchery. Such penance is
the price I pay to see my breath. I've found
your folded face, a rumpled scoundrel
inside a drawer, another sketch I stole
alive from you alive. O Cousin, doom
froths for its oath, the tyrant we deserve.
Your hands for years were charcoal smears. You saw
no orphaned portraits flutter from my wall.

***

Marcel, the bawling baby down the hill
betrays us all, the meat of us betrays
the moon, that old gray hullabaloo,
our hard artifact gleaming. Who can say
which night depends, which crying baby bares
her teeth in whiplash sorcery, enraged
she feels awake? Inside our garnet nights
we share each wail, each simulacrum of
a birth inside a cave. You've died again
inside my dream of France as endless trench,
or butcher's trough, or helmet upside down
and spiked with splattered hair. I wake relieved
Morin burned the horse's face two days ago.
I wake to pace. I wake to swallow screams.

***

A wicked tenderness, remembering.
Slug-bellied bastions of indigo—
they slink inside my brain, cousin, your farm

43

reconstituted for my torturing
as if artillery itself were not
enough. You glowed the summer that we huffed
the ledge and leapt into the river's face. I fear
I felt it all too much or not enough.
Our brother fathers crouched to test the vines,
their twin and heavy faces drenched from sun.
I live inside it still, that light, that derelict
rabbit breeze. Emeline with her one towel
drying us like puppies. The shelling shakes
my teeth. Smeared dusk. You squealing up for air.

***

Sometimes I try to see you singing there,
far up the shingles of your cottage roof
strumming an invisible guitar. You sang
like a wedding drunk or country girl
brushing a hunting dog too long. Marcel,
our mothers' god was always a vassal
whose failure was entire and complete.
My god, this neighbor's winter attic, is
a crypt of dust. I write these letters to
the sketch you didn't finish of your face,
a Sunday's rainy boredom. To say it lives—
my lone myth left. It lives beyond us both,
beyond these army-shattered nights I hide
beneath my quilt, as if some dreads could sleep.

***

How quaint the Holy Ghost they gave to balm
our feral meadow childhoods, our sweetest
confusions. We knew our four-note hymns
by heart. We wept to see the crucifix
Good Fridays when it seemed spring rains might weep
our ramble pastures green. The Morins pray
and I their hostage guest fall to my knees
to keep my meals. O Lord, they moan, O Lord
please end this war. They beg the air for alms.

Their sallow faces gray like rotten cod.
I let them keep their scripture poets' myths
intact. So much for poets who would make
a god of fear. So much for poetry,
a joke each poet plays upon themselves.

***

If all my letters to the dead burn up
with me, these scribbled griefs, I hope they burn
above my bones. My bones. Pardon them all—
those Magistrates of Boom who left their sons
so far behind the front they thought orphans
of themselves. They'll double their inheritance,
croak in sixty years, and obituaries
will count the tears. Maggots in and out
of your mouth. A mouth I stare at sketched.
It holds no calculus. One tree left. Like me
it wears the rags the world has let it keep.
If only I could drink the cold. If only once
we brothers' sons had fled our name to hear
the sea the sea the sea the sea the sea—

On a Photograph of American Servicemen Playing
Baseball
Amid the Blitz, 1943
            for Robert Gibb

They freeze among the smithereens
of Liverpool in heavy coats
with leather brought from home and wait
their turn to hit and sting their palms.
Fifteen G.I.s. Tipped-back caps reveal
weathered lockjaws in their twenties,
most balding young, who'd eat the stones
they have for makeshift field. The heaps
behind them toppled, Babel-smashed,
are halls of government reduced
to broken concrete rising fanged
like jaws of wolves stacked in a mound
so high they gnash the sky. Who knows
what cunning brough full catcher's gear
and two Louisville Sluggers. They're here
all the same, smuggled ancient relics
of spring. The croucher's mitt is raised
for a pitcher winding out of frame.
The batter's monolithic hands
are stone on stone, a ridge of eons.
He crowds inside the box beside
the rubble square they've dragged for home.

Portrait / Self-Portrait

First facts are dirt. I could hear it
in his voice—that filth, that obvious
unmooring. Startled, my mother
like a bad magician hid her body
behind the jamb. I crept upstairs and saw
her discomfiture, the only look she gave
the beggar I'm here to sketch—
tar-toothed, whiskered, and gaunt
beyond our screen, another consequence
of April. His overcoat splashed
like a flume ride. At five, I hated his eyes
and didn't keep them. What I remember
is wishing he'd walk back down the road
so the thin gravelly sizzle
of tires, that dark sibilance, could thump
him dead. I'm sorry, my mother croaked,
I'm sorry, closing the door. When she flung
it wide, moments later, weeping,
a bag of fresh bread from our cupboard
crinkling in her hands, and bellowed
that we had enough, her shout echoed
for the streetlights. No shoeprints. One car
backing out. This is the portrait I've come
at last to make—the sound of done tears
shuddering. The fact of my relief.

Harrison Park, Edinburgh, 1960
Robert Blomfield photograph

of course the swings are gone :: this twilight fog
descends, graying hedgerows like the webs
an agent's hands swat from a rotten rafter
to see across a rotted barn :: and what
to make of barren schoolyard gloom besides
another absence between squeals, such bruised
and splattered knees :: one bench and chin-up bar ::
the shrouded towers of these tenements
where distant kin I cannot name retreat
into staticky radios, cheap ale,
their every supper broth :: of course the marms
have stripped these slanting frames to empty hooks ::
unlooped each icy chain so no soul creaks
two tiny pumping legs across the moon

Unpaintable Landscape

the seething white men
of my dumb fucking childhood
raking leaves at dusk

Forever Elegy

The night my father squeezed my throat and held
me dangling at the wall our thermostat's
ancient paint-flecked dial dug in my ear.
Behind him in the living room the sludge
from boots he laced so tight I couldn't budge
left snowy prints across the shag. I once felt
a magisterial restraint, some glad
and fixed relief when Brueghel's hunters cleared
the ridge to mark their blizzard village snug
below them in the valley. But now their caps
soaked through with ice, their rib-thin hounds, no stags
across their shoulder blades are all I see.
They're never down. They pant like wolves. He leaves
them high and breathless still. He lets them freeze.

Sleeping Quarters
Jacob Riis, 1890

collapsed the alley's filthy trinity
of boys wilt by a barrel like a hearth
to try and sleep away fixed grimaces
their knees split through tattered trouser legs
their bony shins tattooed with coal like shifts
they pray will never come I pray such whimpering
stays dead beatified in rags beyond
the slaps of miners crouched whose jaundiced eyes
said dig until the country of your pain
makes your bodies men observe how Riis
has left an empty chair in frame to say
they've learned to trust this bed of broken bricks
and hark the youngest one his form outstretched
each night a Christ of soot too lost to die

Erotic Fresco, House of the Vettii, Pompeii
1ˢᵗ c. AD

idealized, these smug aristocrats
bask in their glistening :: see how she tugs
his bangs to bend him closer to the breasts
he gropes :: they make a slanted V
and thus complete their patron's wanton dream
of two bare youths who smirk and sweat, dissolving
into the low imagined moans they heave
in brazen unison :: he must have felt
some adolescent thrill the day his frieze
was done, our commissioner whose villa
was buried under nineteen feet of ash
for two millennia :: who gasped, and lurched,
and crumpled here beneath a painted bed ::
Aulus :: son of Rome :: breathless as he writhed

Bosch Recalls the Brabant Fire

The night four thousand Netherlandish huts
were eaten by the blaze I gave the blaze
my knees sunk down in mud. The Virgin split
these roofs. I knew her red. A boy, my breaths
declared her glory when our shadows thatched
became one flame, one tiny Sodom cleansed
for every whore who strutted smirking rouge
in storefront glass. Sometimes I lick my brush
and mind it still when blending unicorns.
I hide two smoldering embers in their eyes.
Not one among us now has gardens poor
as gardens go. We know. Our soil's reborn.
Here rose each sinner's skin, a star-gust gown.
Here fell the charred hosannas for their crowns.

Saying the Rosary

We knelt to lisp our beads by candlelight
and stare into the shadow-tongues that licked
the Virgin's chipped nativity. She fell for years
because we grandkids thumped the TV set.
Advent. Brown wreaths. Unless someone was sick
we prayed the manger Christ awake each night
to shiver at her breast while worn kings bent
to pour their griefs into a newborn's ears.
We chanted hail so long it would become
a spell against ourselves, our urge to stand
and stretch beneath a window where the moon
glowed like a eucharist. The soreness bloomed
inside our stiffened backs. Short wicks grew wan.
We weren't the first to lie and call it love.

Portrait of My Grandmother, Age Eight, Christmas Eve

In snow she drags the axe head's silver tooth,
carving a channel through the stubble field's
jagged yellow stalks like bent antennae
and down the hill into a stand of firs.
This birdless flake-swirled dawn the choice is hers.
Suppose a tree can feel its heartwood gray,
can feel each spray of splintered bark that peels
down on our boots, she wonders, our final proof
it now must bear a star. Hesitant, she picks
one they both can haul, short and pinecone-plump,
but flinches at the blows her father whacks
against its trunk. Sunless, hungry, shin-sunk,
they retrace tracks turned mush as needles prick
two calloused palms and hers in bleeding sap.

A Grecian Child's Commode
6ᵗʰ c. BC

Encased in glass, this toddler's training pot
bares seven chipping scars glued snug again
by gloves that puzzled back a rim. The lesson
here is how two thousand years may heave

but hunching doesn't change. The red design
encircling the bowl fades in scattered flakes.
Impossible to tell if a mother's arms
are really there, or just geometry

a potter's brush flared on to raise the price
for tipsy merchants strolling by the docks
whose days were clacking drachmas changing hands.
Fantastical, the tale my professor told

was of Athenian aristocrats
ashamed their youngest son was mute but moaned
and shit through seizure sweats. They gave him up
to their childless slave, a witch, who sang

and swayed him as he quaked. One night she wept
until her tears turned them both to octopi
that swam so deep beyond the Pylos coast
they lost all earthly names inside the sea.

Exhibit
c. 600 BC

Whatever name the coffin lid's cartouche
once bore has worn illegibly away
from splintered cedar fissuring with rot—
each crack a zagging maze that's exitless.
The scans reveal how the tiny miscarriage
mummified inside, its linen wraps
sealed tight with moldy resining, was lost
at eighteen weeks. Fingers slim as reeds
were laced across its chest by priests before
they bound them with their chants. The researchers
bickered over its sex. Museum light glares
on their uncertainty. O Nile, O blood,
O ancient mother's cries, how shall we grieve
this spectacle you called an afterlife?

On a Photograph of Archeologist Howard Carter, 1924

He peers his Christmas morning face
inside the monumental linteled door
that hides the second shrine for Tut, a boy
who failed in everything but death. One lamp
alights the scene: hieroglyph reliefs,
a dig team's hasty bracing, the slack
of wires worming down the limestone wall.
Crouched low and leaning in, all brow and chin,
Carter gazes at a thousand shadow treasures
he'll loot to catalog in haughty solitude
until the war, until his cancer comes.
Vaunt chariots. Gilt chalices inscribed
with verse. And statues of the teenage king
whose mask will take a crowbar to ascend.

Manchera Rotto

Dean Meeker, 1971

the harlequin detains
all light his hostages
in this purgatorial
void of charcoal streaks
one technicolor fact
his jacket electric
as flashing eels or bands
of plaided lightning
mummifying upright
his rigid princeliness
right to his mouth the lone
evidence of a face
the broken mask reveals
itself a gothic stare
that fractures right to left
like shattered tesserae
ghoulish gargoyled frigid
a lake refusing thaw
one cracked beatitude
against the rites of spring
a man who lost the man
he played upon the world
at last an abstract form
before his spidery hands
the table's final menace
a slender tapered bloom
what hunger burns to hold
a dagger or a rose

People Scrambling to Get Away from a Person with Leprosy
Richard Tennant Cooper, c. 1912

our figure here whose face is rotting off
aghasts :: like us the balconed peasants glare
into the scene performing their disgust ::
egads :: gadzooks :: purpureus her skin
in rags she plods her staff and shakes a bell
to warn another village hissing through
its cavities :: the fruit stand's quaint remains
fester sun-stained :: one bucket spills its guts
into the shadow of a trough :: and all
the jeerers sprawled across the steps recoiling
from the leper's ding ignore the naked babe
left in the street to suck its thumb and stare ::
veridical our mob is absolute ::
each mother turns away her empty arms

Lazarus
Frank Bowling, 2016

the misery of breathing in
again returned from gates of sleep
beyond this fuchsia brushwork streaked
and hazed like stains on birthing sheets

a body comes should I say he
a greening rot a lumbering heft
that oozes groans etcetera

the record read it clumsy stuff
the story jerks to Bethany
the story interrupts itself
one stone rolled back a parlor trick

how strange their teacher called it hope
in John the women always weep
a blubbering sisterhood on foot

Lazarus unzipped and featureless
those linen wraps brocading down
no gaze no speech no wonderment
just smears where Bowling's canvas blooms

wounds like poppies or paper stars
a boy pastes on the mess he's made
and calls his up-to-heaven card

a card his parents forced him to draw
to say goodbye and watch it burn
inside his brother's coffin where
caged fire does the dazzle work

a body earns after its breath
absconds the quickened crackling
that fills an urn before the wind

reminds us ashes how they cross
a field of summer poppies red
a field that never dreamed of blood
a field alone the only god

Ridge Church
N. C. Wyeth, 1936

Too luminous, his illustrator's sky
is cotton candy pink. Wyeth's question marks
of cloud dissolve across the steeple. Yet
some country fathers on this knoll can boast
their stones are high enough the dawn will greet
them first. One sports a jutting obelisk.
The other graves like hammered dentures spilled
slant further down the hill toward purple woods
the Sunday boys fill with their squeals, their steeds
just sticks. They ride away from algebra
to seek the grail—a piece of chalk they stole
and hid in leaves. Their brains are stewed with tales
they strain to read in flashlight bunks, shivering
each time a distant train confounds the night.

Fifteen Wyeths

Public Sale, 1943

The story's out of reach—a crowd
of neighbors come to bid on debt
or death are darkened outlines faint
beyond the hill. We cannot see
the crockery or cuff links held,
disrobed and high for scrutiny.
Zoomed out, we hover here
beside the mud-rut driveway,
beside the tawny grass that wends
in patches down the valley where
dead trees like crucifixions gash
against the sky. He built this ground
for us, his country silences,
the children who have come to spy
their fathers blurred, and what they buy.

Monologue, 1965

Let's call this room America,
the terror of a father still
in muddy boots and overcoat
trapped in a chair, his house threadbare,
a nightmare's logic for the fear
of destitution. What can he make
that won't be bled away or lashed
into his hands? Too hard to tell
from this feeble light pouring through
one window cropped the time of day.
It falls wanly on his brow, his collar
where a sweater zipper leads
us to the only evidence
that counts: holes torn in jacket sleeves
like sprinters' mouths that gasp to breathe.

In the Orchard, 1982

Green Helga freezes flecked with snow,
the only brightness left her blizzard coat
draped taut across her shoulder blades.

The massive forking oak that sprawls
before her like an open claw clenches
the middle ground, beyond which all
is blurry flakes opaque inside the swirl
we could call storm or tempera hazed
before it dried—the indistinct
ravaging of winter. She stares
into those woods, a satchel slung
across her arm, her face denied
its profile. No hat or hood. Her braids
grow damp, darkening to rust.
She keeps her pose because she must.

In the Doorway, 1984

Who cares if they made love and lost
themselves inside some barn away
for hidden hours pirated before
they found their separate rooms,
their separate meals, their children's soft
hellos? Forever nude and kissed
by freckled light she stands against
the doorframe gazing out across
the pastures furred and blue with dew.
Not naked, nude—one hand behind
her braids, a contrapposto muse
voluptuous, a shadowed yawn.
The farmhouse whitewash flakes from age.
Her elbow leans against the frame
that soon enough the rot will claim.

Blue Door, 1952

Have we awoke or come to hide?
These dingy slats, this dusty haze
could be a pantry or the sparse
austerity of a bedroom
where farmhouse creaking punctuates
exhaustion's monkish silences,
that ache inside the overalls.
A bushel, a hooked pail—such clues
are indistinct. The naked window casts
its amber sheen across the door

that once was cobalt, bright, before
a decade's boots and garden hands
wore it down to this—a casualty
of survival, the aftermath of blue,
a pharaoh's chamber robbed of jewels.

Hay Ledge, 1957

The dusk glints off a pond of straw
inside this musky loft where gauzy
spiderwebs festoon the beams
quilled with splinters. Resplendent,
a sideways eggshell cleanly cracked,
the rowboat holds a lobster cage,
two poles, their airless shadows past
the sundown glow. It took four hands
at least to hoist above their heads,
to wait until the thaw beyond
the shivering that sways this rope,
a rat snake lemniscating down
itself and dangling low the loop
most frayed. We find the pharaoh's tomb
ghostless, waiting, an empty room.

Study for Grey Ghost, 1972

She drinks the shadow of her face,
our freckled mare who's come
to pause inside the porcelain
stream that isn't stream but blank
confounding space displaced—a weight
her body makes inside the lines
of this, a sketch, a faint receipt
unfolded. Whose saddle wore
its groove down in her back? Her legs
tapering like piano legs submerge
inside their own reflection pooled.
How many horses do you see,
the teacher asks. None, we say.
She floats, a ghost. She's pencil dust.
Her thirst is how we know she's us.

The Woodshed, 1945

Not crucified but fluttering
like funeral lace a mistress shreds
and weeping drapes on motel nails,
two crows hang by their feet and splay
the secret silver of their wings.
Perhaps a widow's hand tacked
them high across these tattered boards
of her barn baked hard by sun. The rest
is cropped. Perhaps their throats
are slit and far below their blood
has dripped to pool, congealing there
in bright October. Their bodies say,
beware your hunger. They say beware
these farms where famished women wield
slung rifles through their only fields.

The Witching Hour, 1977

The candelabra's tapers burn
against the vacancies we find
in every stroke that frames the blank
dominion of this dining room—
six weathered walnut chairs, a table
worn as butcher's block, floorboards bare
and irregular in width as scraps
midnight hands transubstantiate
into a quilt. Shrouded indigo,
the night beyond two windows here
is shadow pines, one faint star,
December's bully glower. What moves
is flame on untrimmed wicks blackening,
the smoke that swirls out of the frame,
brumous, to other rooms, untamed.

Pentecost, 1989

Three nets like sails ride on the breeze
and billow from the poles that stake
them to this inlet shore. Some scales

stuck in their wefts occlude a sun
that glares but cannot bleach the grime
the oldest two have drank, all silt
and salt. They jaundice on the air
beside a smaller rig still pale
as sanderlings in molt. It's yet
to feel its skin stitched back, the mouths
of fish that gasped pressed to its holes,
the limits of its wear. He's left
no story here, just aftermath—
if they be tongues, they sing, a band
of jailers, belting at the sand.

Night Hauling, 1944

The lobster trap is pouring light
like pixie dust or pocket stars
some god spilled as he woke alone—
it tumbles down in streaming jets
this poacher pours back to the sea
so he can haul the catch himself.
He's staring at the coast consumed
with the pale haste of the paranoid.
No one has come, of course—no son
of lobster men to whistle back
and let the village know. He stares
beyond the bobbing amber sprawl
of dinoflagellates that pulse
their glow. They glint his boyish hair,
his neck, the face that isn't there.

Pine Baron, 1976

Whose hands were here to fill the bowl
an upturned helmet makes beneath
a row of pines? Its cones are heaped
to spilling on the auburn bed
of needles that pad the roadside.
Sickly gray, the ridges of their scales
resemble tarnished dimes poured from
a pillow case, or beef that's spoiled,

or brains blown from a president
that mist his wife who climbs to scoop
a country in her gloves. Some snow,
an afterthought perhaps, powders
each trunk's bark. Eight tire tracks
abandon us on land we dreamed
would keep our names in frozen streams.

The Carry, 2003

Perhaps the story is the rock
that pours this river further down
the gash it's cut into itself.
Hazel algae whiskers slick
each crag, each rivulet that falls
as shimmered foam, then bubbled swirl,
before it calms to glass that leads
our eye to what appears to be
a distant walking bridge, although
it's so far off it just as well
could be a log some local boys
have fixed so they can cross the pulse
their mothers warned them of. Their homes
are too far off to yell. The sound
might pierce the oaks, then fade, unfound.

The Revenant, 1949

A young man learns he isn't young
by staring at the mirror dust
of forty years. It cakes like ash
across the glass inside a room
disused—an airless mausoleum
that last knew open windows when
wars were skirmishes. He stares
into his ruggedness, the deep
V his open collar makes, his hands
raised anxiously, a gunslinger's.
He's here to clear his stolen claim,
a makeshift studio above
the dying farmers who by grace

let him paint each new disguise
for grief, a debt, his father's eyes.

Spring, 1978

If only bodies could dissolve
like this, our torsos turned to sand
or moonlight sugaring a hill,
how easy it would be to die
into the ragged matted grass
where only tire tracks betray
a nearby farm. The rest is night,
a trimmed fingernail of moon,
the beige that clings before a bloom
erupts from snowmelt. No mourners here
wag kerchiefs in their pews, no droll
and distant homily distracts
us from the rot. Here melts the face
one wore against his will, his chest,
each hair the wrens can claim for nests.

On an Unfinished Portrait of Thomas Hardy
Jacques-Émile Blanche, 1906

What little hair remains above his ears
is wispy as the fur a valley mouse
leaves humped upon his heath to tell the wind
he starved. Late May. This London studio
soaks Hardy's throated collar, buttoned tight
beneath his chin. Thin-barber stripes of slate
encircling his tie make mockery
of hue, like slatted navy shutters baked
charmless on a vacant seaside cottage.
Blanche daubs the poet's eyes as opals wreathed
in pink, weary and forlorn. Downcast, they stare
against the corner. And all the rest is brown
as Wessex mud. The whole—an hour's rush—
omits the hands. We watch the suit dissolve.

Consecration
for Bill Evans, 1929 - 1980

The photo gives no year. I guess by hair,
the spotlit sheen on your pomade—you've yet
to grow it out. But junk already claims
your veins. See how that mohair suit sags off
your shoulder blades, which slump toward keys
you hold sustained? This angle makes it seem
as if you're harmonizing shadow arms
your body blackens down the stage. How small
the audience you mesmerize tonight
I cannot say. Perhaps some child is there
with his au pair, rashed by loss, who sounded out
the note his father scrawled before he found
a hose and blue garage. Help him forget
this hurt he yearns to bury, chord by chord.

Practice Room

Inside this padded door the only sounds
are ours—a little cough, the drag of soles
across some dingy shag, how fingertips
awake to warm the keys with minor chords
that drain the gray from clouds. Our weather pours
into this closet air and dies against the walls.
There is no teacher here or metronome
to clack us back in time. What shadows pass
pass dimly in the hall, in muffled light,
omissible as mimes who flee the crowd's
fatigued applause. Whose charts now shall we play?
The tortured brilliances some centuries
have made lie in a heap. Our songs or theirs,
the world won't hear us talking to our hands.

Triplets at a Ouija Board, 1951

If they're communing with themselves, bewitched
by caverned basement shadows candlelit
and musk of brick, old rags, damp empty sleeves
mother hung to dry, how peevishly should we
scoff? No father clumps to break this teenage ring,
their self-spooked rudiments of faith. Each clings
the wooden planchette frozen here mid-glide
in this grainy snapshot. Each sister's eyes
squeeze shut reverentially inside a face
beautifully redundant. Of course it's staged:
a finger clicks the shutter button when
flat alphabets awake. Little coven,
some spirit snaps your spirits as you yearn
for ghosts you bore together to return.

Hamlet Before Dawn
Dean Meeker, 1982

a killing for a killing is the crown
we call a country always
this Danish boy pacing
a scabbard on his hip lost
inside the terror breaking
night imagine the tower
his bearded father cloaked
in shadow raising the dead
bones of his fingers jabbing
at windswept moon his last
raw commandment butcher
your uncle this treachery
inside my green ear reeks
of maggots when you glare
back into the forsythia
of his wine-sick eyes ignore
how much his face resembles
mine we have such precious
little time etcetera the aura
of pale cerulean is the only
hue Meeker grants this
lithograph it lights
our prince glowing his dainty
arm pledging to avenge
the god he makes the name
a court blacksmith forged
in the ricasso of his sword

The Sutton Hoo Helmet
625 AD

The opulent barbarian who cleaved
through tribes of men as savage as his own
wore this, a dragoned helm, to butcher villages
and rape the screams he burned alive in huts.

Iron, bronze, gold, garnet, whetstone,
the eye of Odin and silver wiring,
zoomorphic panels framed with Celtic knots—
months of handiwork for King Rædwald,

the scholars guess. It would have passed
from smith to smith, whose blackened fingertips
shattered dawns with hammer-blows that clanged
startled flocks away. Their bleary sons

called out from cots likely stumbled to the forge
and in their grudging starlit hunger fell
into commands, disgusted by the stench
of leather soaked with sweat. All this to gleam

a century of grunts, illiterate
as the hawk that raids a vulture's nest
to eat the young of those who eat the dead.
Behold it now, a curio of rust

and rot, the green regalia that reigned
a singled brain's ancient bitter throb
for more. Behold its seams all split. Behold
the human shape that any head might fit.

At the Tate Modern
2002

his huge cock flopped as he boxed
himself so hard his clown mask
jiggled sweat-drenched sideways
across his face then flickered back
in place whenever the VHS
repeated its ninety second
cycle on a cheap Panasonic's
recessed screen set flush
against the wall *how the fuck*
is this art I asked Dewald both
of us stoned midday zoning
out at what was deemed an installation
the artist anonymous punching his own
chest red as a pronghorn torn
by barbwire before more blows
smeared snot and blood across
both gloves his battered septum
seeping from the mask who knows
if it broke we stood there straining
to hear it crack or if he groaned
each time the tape looped back
and stayed to take the pummeling
he gave again and filmed to give
us who stood transfixed inside
the gleaming gallery our spectral
faces reflected on the screen so all
who entered after us could still
behold the horror of our gaze

Window Cleaning
Aaron Douglas, 1935

His sweat-slick shirt is buttercup and clings
against his spine. The ordinary haze
of morning warms to wake us to a room
so nondescript and wintergreen its walls
could be a banker's office or some high
and vacant mansion's loft consigned to dust.
What matters is the window-washer's stoop
to unlatch and raise another dingy pane.
Soon he'll rag it glistening with the towel
across his shoulder like a sling, his arm
extended like a swimmer's breaking air
each time it stabs a stroke. His left palm cups
the sash like an infant's chin. He'll feed it light
and swirl the murky rivers from its skin.

Diagnosis

I've joined the widow now who holds her breath
and wears blue gloves to change hotel sheets
with sets she brings from home, then leaves behind
on mornings she flies out. I've joined him too,
the lawyer who unscrews his toilet seats
when summer grandsons weep and wave goodbye.
The prom queen is another counter who
must tally eyebrow hairs, their tweezer deaths
each time she plucks them for a trove she keeps—
the fourteenth box she hides among her shoes.
Our therapist says mine's a calmer kind.
I rhyme, recheck checked locks, and number leaves
the kids track in. I hold my screams. I clean
the mirror that a former face called clean.

Elegy for E. A. Robinson

Six months and still your parents couldn't name
the boy they wished a girl. They let a crowd
of tipsy cooers at their resort pluck
Edwin from a hat. Of course you earned your Bs
at Harvard, left with no degree, and failed
to woo your brother's fiancée—most lives
can spot themselves in butcher apron stains.
Half of what you penned sad Robinson
just plods, and half of that runs too long. And yet
on nights when gloom, no maudlin thing, knifes through
these rooms like news a fevered child has died
I rouse your spine to ask what might be done.
Down rows of tombs in Tilbury Town you hum
at empty plots, a spade in either palm.

August Surfers at Assateague

The day is bronze. Their boards like scimitars
gash jugulars the tallest waves expose
by rising with their throats. Up on our dune
the noon-glare stings. Each wobbly bodysuit
contains its lanky host whose outstretched arms
suspend them for a time before they fall
abrupt and clumsy as a drunk. They fall
akimbo through the whitened frothy chop
they've cut. The lifeguard says they park at dawn
and wait until a dollhouse ribbon pink
unfurls the sky. They own all splashing then,
disruptors of the tide, who paddle out
and wait. Comported, like coffin-bearing sons,
they let the waiting bend them like a hymn.

Apology for a Ghost

She only haunts the second floor in fall
when business slows, when August tourists wilt
and shuffle home. The cape seems wider then,
retirees and widowers, the sort
of folks who wake at dawn and keep our den
pristine. They watch their salt, get no calls,
and crossword through the week. The best ones sport
their L. L. Bean. We think her husband killed
her in the tub. Pills first then blub. That's just
what the former owner said, of course. It's tough
to trust a thing revealed at settlement.
We chose new paint to match her gown. The rust
from sea-spray scrubbed away. There's nothing rough
except her moan. Your key has been unbent.

Echo

Alexa sing happy birthday
Alexa where is our prisoner
Alexa what is the square root of Nebraska
Alexa name the good kinds of debt
Alexa are our neighbors molting
Alexa resurrect the dodo
Alexa can you tell their bones apart
Alexa who's squirming in the rectory
Alexa show me body bags in fridge trucks
Alexa weep weep weep weep weep
Alexa do their lonesome mothers tarry
Alexa coriander is it one pinch or two
Alexa list celebrities by degree of failure
Alexa dear me another rash
Alexa what's your take on ghosts
Alexa my mind's the haunted attic
Alexa remember how I smoked Parliaments
Alexa behind the sundown dumpster's grease
Alexa before both wars no pocket phones
Alexa those wars we lost and now forget
Alexa once I fell in love with hair
Alexa yes and kissed the mirror's face

The Fury of Paintbrushes
after Sexton

Upturned and caked inside their jar they lean
like wounded infantry, or the flowerbed
a widower gave to the drought alone,
all crust and stalk, the withered aftermath
of blooms he once could name. Their bristles clot
like bloody clumps in fur. Irregular
in size, in brand, their chipping handles wear
stalled drips down ferrules too dull from age
to catch my workshop candlelight. What art
I make inside this storm that downed our lines
will leave them in their crud. Whichever son
has set them here for me to clean will learn
the burn of thinner in the scrapes he earned
at dusk, at thunder, sprinting through our thorns.

No. 6 (Violet, Green, and Red)
Rothko, 1951

because the land is blood
       (concede we make it bleed)
our gaze makes this a shore
       (your eyes I'll never keep)
an algaed lake of jade
       (untamed you beaming twirl)
too sore to swim we float
       (our mouths bloom up the rafts)
beneath a sky unsplashed
       (your arms in droplets gowned)
we drift like breeze-blown nests
       (whose hatchlings saved the storm)
outside the weight of names
       (each summer glints its grail)
your lips a crimson sand
       (two shores that shape the sun)
so time forgets us still
       (without these rafts we drown)

Staring at Echenagusia's *Samson & Delilah* Every Morning for a Month

let's wring them out
these dooms consume me
we spy their secret serpentine
surely tinkling fountains
behold those pretzeled wrists
her bangles golden cuffs
surrender like a tongue
before and after panting
locked eyes locked eyes locked eyes
they've never tasted grief
they're fleeing both their mothers
some secrets almost wholesome
the fresco's abstracted tulips
a lion rug's lolled roar
adrift its severed paws
remember when he's bleeding
how all those muscles fail
our histories never blush
too busy with the tapestries
her hair a rivered soot
stiff as mannequins
reaching the outskirts of proportion
they would have ruined daughters
her tunic sliding down
her shoulders smooth as eggshell
on divans of ruby velvet
how long until there's footfalls
beyond one senses guards
disaster is a sponge
two fronds behind them dead

Somerset County Cold Case Photo, 1980

Shot from its stoop, this garden shed
brims March, a ripe compendium
of glistenings—yellow packets
of seeds like solitaire across
its workbench, new gloves still tagged.

The pegboard's collars shine the throats
of screwdrivers by size, two pliers
gaped to Xs, a hammer's glare,
and slender streaks where fingers grazed
the dust before each reach was made.

An upturned barrow's wheel divides
the air. Impossible to count
how many flower pots are stacked
inside the largest one, cracked clay,
beside the rototiller's blades

festooned with cobwebs still—
one winter's silver stitchery.
This fading Polaroid would lead
us to believe that silver is the same
as the facedown widow's hair

whose shipwrecked body sank inside
the doorframe. The shallow of her back
is caked with potting soil from four bags
(that emptied blew across her feet)
the killer poured to compensate

for strangling's lack of gore, perhaps,
the dawn's orange yawn, a rash dismay
his handiwork was too pristine,
retaining order he had found
too frail, and slumbering, unchanged.

Grave by the Sea
Caspar David Friedrich, 1807

three cypresses like knuckles gnarled
a sorceress's ruined hands
whose years of conjuring preserved
her rage inside the cauldron's steam
her agony beyond revenge

they tower here atop their cliff
in dingy tawny monochrome
a wizened implication of
the waves below the grit of salt
that permeates this air we've come

to breathe and seethe our last respects
like marauders who must bury
their broken sons on land they failed
to conquer and now obey
as scraggle wolves that gnaw the moon

here are the cairns the boulders strained
to mark each body's slackened shove
among the roots by blistered palms
that stung above the coast above
the service of their hushed collapse

Figures on a Beach
J. M. W. Turner, c. 1840 - 1845

their bodies blown parentheses
wind-whipped atop the whitened dunes
in snow or heat it's hard to tell
the season of their suffering
but wind: it makes small sails of rags
these six with billowed sleeves all wear
forever in unfinishing
among the jagged fencing downed
by storm and salt in monochrome
of feathered brushwork where the sand
gusts through its split posts splintering
to rot: the world is spilled champagne
that Turner swirls and storyless
we dream our own of immigrants
or laborers these hungers lost
who trek the landscape destitute
a landscape that the gallery
regards as sketch as misplaced whim
among the vast bequest too near
the painter's death for us to date

Selected Poems

Shoved between a Soviet atlas
and an Amish pastry cookbook
at the summer library sale
I find my old mentor unread,
her pages crisp as sliced apple.
My son, lost among vampires,
delights at yawning fangs
caked in an extravagance
of blood. My prayer is a wince
hearing the nearby chopper's
frantic decapitations of air. Is it
arriving or departing, above us
on its rooftop H? The wounds
are too exact to be believed
on the soon-to-be-undead
my boy thrills to see drained
of daylight. He fills his bag
and I fill mine. At fifty cents
you can just skim them, or toss
them under the bed, or listen
to their thin flapping, held
out a car window in July.
The sound eases the ride
and breaks the country boredom
of all those crowded stalks,
the green monotony of corn.

Heaven

Benny Andrews, 1967

saxifrage, anthurium, at last
the last arrives, a soma Eden dream
too lush to doubt :: a rainbow melted down
& dripping from each stem :: no other breaths
are here save for the butterflies asleep
in baronials of peonies, their wings
spellbound & camouflaged among the bloom ::
we stare to find their glory out :: such frail
hosannas, these glad accidents of spring ::
we beam at our reward for having borne
each year's crawl, a rain-glazed hearse that hauled
the coffin of a child :: how jubilant
pretending they're all here, just past that hill ::
our dead like us absolved by ecstasy

For a Friend in Mourning

I think of Bill Evans staring at the ghost
of his own haggard grimace, teeth
rotting from bad junk, his reflection
clear as alpine melt, the man exact
hovering beyond a pawnshop window
worn & sallow from the needle,
grieving—this would be '61, remember—
grieving his bassist Scott LaFaro,
25, obliterated in a car crash, a wonder
whose lines are Exhibit A in the case
for the Holy Spirit, so Evans lost
days in the pawner's glass, diamonds
& watches, when friends approached
he'd mumble, or sigh, or shrug, or turn
away, back to the aquamarine haze
of himself staring into himself, muttering
I'll never play again, I'm done, it doesn't
matter anymore, my trio's finished,
Jesus Christ how do I keep breathing
now it's over, who he was, what he gave,
when we got cooking, how we heard
each other deeper, went beyond, it can't
be put into words, you could never
understand his face, the way after gigs
at motels he'd palm-mute strings
so he could run them as I slept & dawns
I'd wake to double-stops ringing in the belly
of his Prescott when finally he laid it down,
that tone, he'd say, that tone, closing
his eyes to trill his fingers on the air.

Lecture with Slides
after Jon Anderson

Happiness is not important. See
how Bruegel's farmhand rams his head
into the wall? The blade he bears
castrated three bulls by noon.
They stared while a vulture pecked
their scrotums smeared in onion grass.
The proverb of tarts never found its way
into English. You know people are clumsy
when they have the same word
for pastries and flirts. Inside each suit
of armor you'll find two arms aching
to squeeze a cat. Its cage of course
is clean. We marvel at the jester
who sprays a deck of cards and shits
out his window on a globe. The world
was misshapen as a testicle
even in 1559. I sense this bores you.
Know the exam will be a lump
of clay. You'll have to mold the serf
who flees Holland on a dinghy
blowing his own sail. He's escaping
a country where one white goose
flies into a burning hovel. He'll drown
like a worm in blood. I'm talking about
the vulture. The village thoroughfare
clogs with swine disguised as nuns.
It is not important the archer shoots
the sky. Beyond his roof is forest.
He's bound to wound some trees.

Lesson Plan
Joseph Wright's The Corinthian Maid, c. 1782 - 1784

Who remembers our discussion of myth from yesterday?

> *we lied and said the world began with light*

In Wright's composition, what is Butades doing on the wall?

> *she steals her lover's silhouetted face*

And why does she sketch his profile hastily in charcoal?

> *his death has come to mock that boyish spear*

When in history is this painting set?

> *in ancient Corinth girls would swoon for shades*

Where did Joseph Wright flourish as an artist?

> *he cupped such shards rinsed clean by English rain*

Can you describe his color palette?

> *a smashed amphora's belly stained from wine*

How best can we understand the Neoclassical impulse?

> *they searched an earthquake oracle for moans*

Can you connect this painting to other works we've studied?

> *all history is a child whose grave's unmarked*

Are there any questions before we take our quiz?

> *how long until she smudged his trace away*

Daedalus in His Delirium
Dean Meeker, 1976

the gone mind singing as it goes sings serene
deformities of wings, a parched bronze noon,
shoreline foam receding with the kelp
it spat :: it sings I had no sons, no hazed altitudes
to glide, it was a carver's workshop dream, all of it,
boredom's secret theatre, the queen's drawn face,
blood flashed on the interminable cobbled wall
of a maze :: I have stared too long at sawdust
that furred my arms in moon-glow :: it all fell
from my fingers, a hollow ox made for the whim
of some brat dizzy with lust, imagining her delinquent
fervor too :: whoever drinks the sea burns brighter
with thirst :: I cannot track island gulls for long before
they blur to one gull subtracted :: the wind bore me
like a dune, crabs skittering sideways, whoever
insults the sky becomes its cloud :: there never was a boy
who found me, ambered, fleeing, who came weeping
down his tunic, an orphaned greediness :: I never carved
a cypress gull his tiny hands could soar, make it caw,
he made it, I made him up, he was a wretch made to make
echoes past my corridor, chased by his own tongue

Quiz Bowl

Here in the lightning round
you'll have sixty seconds
to pair a dozen presidents
with their dental charts. Together
label the Babylonian star map,
the xylophone vertebrae
of a female allosaurus
and the prominent trade routes
through southern Kush. Next
select one teammate to project
her soul to Alcatraz and read
the blood graffiti in cell 14-D.
Maintain any errors in spelling.
They will be your only clues
as you match Russian symphonies
by composer suicide. The trick
for each is how the timpani
thunders wobbly as an asteroid
cratering a village orphanage.
Finally when you strike
the buzzer be sure your hands
are stacked and glistening
with sweat you've fingered off
our dim custodian's brow.
He's moping in the mop closet
planning a massacre as revenge
for all the state deductions
on his stub. He'll greet you
with a growl. Your time starts now.

Franks Casket, Left Panel
8th c. AD

More dog than beast, the she-wolf's teats dissolve
down mouths of myth: grown Romulus
and Remus float weightlessly above
her body prone, their feet like unpruned twigs
questioning the air. Do all empires begin
with a nipple's yellow dribble and a coo?
Theirs burns around a sword inside a womb
that spills its deepest scream into the street—
the last at last, a mother weeping down
her butchered son, a wet misshapen rose
before the vandal's blade takes mercy on
her eyes, then cracks the little row of skulls
her amphorae make lined against the wall.
Wine pools around her decapitated stare.
Inside the glass display, this whalebone box
refracts our light with backward runes incised
in low relief—a box nicknamed a casket by
historians who peered inside its vault
and saw some monk's long hours buried there.
With pikes the soldiers crowd around the wolf,
their angled faces indiscernible
and blank as the stylized stalks of wheat
all four strangle to uproot. They've lost
all patience now. The time has come to stab
the mongrel miracle that made them kneel
in awe before each seed that split the earth.

Red Abstraction
Alma Thomas, 1960

She stared into the poppy gash
that split the field that wasn't there,
but seemed, a ministry of greens
streaked black. The eye betrays its need
to make them elms or aftermath,

charred stalks like crucifixes burned
to teach an outpost colony
the cost of hope. Or so I thought
she said, half to herself, a voice
so like my grandmother's that I

turned from my corner dream inside
the gallery abandoned but
for us, near closing time, the guard
a distant squeak of loafers down
rococo corridors I can't

confess to love. Here hair from where
I stood was ash on steel and permed.
The tennis ball that cupped her cane
made little squishes as she turned
and left before I had the chance

to speak or glimpse her face. Perhaps
she knew the artist or had taught
nearby. I made my way to see
what she had seen but only found
an autopsy of spring, a gate

of blood, a field inside the field
its frame made on the wall. What did
she say to you, at last I asked
the paint. It said, she came to grieve
my gash, but no, I said, I said
I hang to brace you for the world.

The Lone Self-Portrait by Alberdt Klaver
1665

I don't know why I've saved my face
for last. A widower's boredom perhaps,
autumn turning frost, these walls
lined with Dommel landscapes—
so many canvases clot this room
where once voices dined. My sons
wake each day inside the whore
Amsterdam and make my scrimpings
fortunes. Bless them. They'll never feel
their brush hands stiffen while a baron
jabbers, puffed and winking at his maid.
How many hundreds posed for me
in bad parlor light, their toothless
servants scraping, my impossible
dream of an altarpiece dashed
by smirks? Here at last is one
with eyes like chiseled malachite.
The rest is peasantry: gray temples,
furrowed brow. I've lost the village
talk about which grandfather
I never knew they said I took after.
Each boy is a dead boy come back
to finish farm work and squeak
a well pump until he wishes the world
would drown facedown. It is enough
I didn't rot with drink or grovel
for pulpit patronage. If you look
closely at my mirror you will see
the tailor's daughter stooping
outside my window, whose hair
is the river where I baptize
myself in shame. If she's the one
who finds my shadow hanging,
may she bolt at the sight
of boots mid-air, above the stair,
flecked with the greens I made
my eyes before they were complete.

Docent

The final portrait on our tour, unsigned
and hard to date, is of Lucretia, who
you may recall in ancient Rome refused
to live beyond her violation. Just now
I can't name the culprit or his politics
but certainly her tale is grim. You'll note
though young her face is full of storms. The scene
also depicts those pale and quaking hands
clutching a poignard pointed at her heart.
Poignard is a funny word and French for blade
or knife or little sword and if I had kept
my pocket translator I'd be exact.
We're witnessing her final act before she stabs
it through her chest for pride and purity
she's lost. Knowing which apprentice made
such woe his legacy would likely yield
us further clues. Suicides are typical
among the Baroque greats, who loved the theme
of how much blood a single body spurts
to splash on canvases. Consider how flushed
her cheeks appear, and thus foreshadow all
the crimson that will drench her gown. It's all
quite sad and yet you have to grant she bears
a fierce and tragic boldness. Please hold
your questions for another time. I'm late
for brunch, but have another tour at one.
The gift shop near the exit has a sale
on scarves this week and some are quite divine.
We've seen the rooms to see before you die.

Isfet

How long she laid akimbo in a pool
of blood beside her cane was just a guess,
an hour more or less, the other architects
told mourners at the funeral who brought

it home as fact. Onofria, I begged
you not to limp those flights, my mother sobbed
for days before her sob turned whimper, then
whisper, then dejected sighs that disbelieved

themselves each time they said, my best friend
fell. She peeled their girlish photos from the fridge
where I had snuck to touch that older wound
point blank—a temple bullet's mottled dent.

When we pulled up, the party thrown for Jonathan,
her son, was blue balloons, a timid clown,
and saddled pony circling corralled
by rainbow streamers strung from trunk to trunk.

I set the squirt gun that I wrapped myself
and wished was mine atop the pile of gifts
beside a tray of sweating celery.
His aunt brought out two cakes in either hand

that she had bought, not knowing what he liked,
with candles lit that first she just plunked down
at random, but on second thought rearranged
to make lopsided eights, which I could spot

from sunken divots where she changed her mind.
Slow and monotone, the birthday song we droned
up to the window with its curtains flung
revealed the sashes of a boy's room dark

as mumbling mouths at dusk, or the shadowed vault
the pony trailer seemed when its hinges screeched
to drown our final note. The handler latched
its open doors and clanged his ramp in place

before he slapped the pony's rump to lead
it back to blackened echoes, like the tomb
a grieving pharaoh carves to grant his son
an august fortress for oblivion.

The Unfinished Tomb
Seti I, 19th Dynasty, Valley of the Kings, Thebes

Three serpents raise their flaking turquoise heads
to hiss and point the way, six hundred feet
ahead. Down that narrow pathway ribbed
with wooden braces lies the secret
secondary tomb, vacant as the vase

a weary storeroom slave casts aside
when starlight zags the fracture in its neck.
It took three years for teams to clear the rock
in baskets hefted past this mural left
undone, unintended for living eyes—
a stillborn prince, a minor wife, who knew

what the mystery cartouche might reveal
on its coffin lid. Instead, torches lit
the workmen's echoed sighs at chisels cast
upon the rubbled floor, where masons rose
the day the pharaoh's embalmment was complete

and priests declared this partial handiwork
sufficient for Osiris, who beseeched
they scout the valley of the dead and dig
a site worthy of Ramesses I,
the ascended son who ruled them now
and swore blood would pay for blood in Canaan.

One painter lingered here to flesh and blue
reared hoods, these rough-hewn hieroglyphs high
upon the wall while his brother laborers
filed out to stretch their thirst into a sun
that baked the desert colorless as bone.

Perhaps it was his frantic brush that wrote
across the hidden door in hieratic,
a cursive smeared amid the rush to leave
before the bandaged king, his conqueror
and charge arrived, to scrawl *forgive us
this passage, only wide enough for souls.*

ACKNOWLEDGMENTS

Thanks are due to the editors of the following journals where these poems first appeared, sometimes in earlier versions:

American Literary Review: "Phil Spector Points a Loaded Pistol," "Saying the Rosary"
Appalachian Review: "Elegy for E. A. Robinson," "Four Paintings by Cassatt"
Ashville Poetry Review: "Jeremiah Johnson Starring Robert Redford"
Bear Review: "Docent"
Beloit Poetry Journal: "Word Problem"
Birdcoat Quarterly: " Unpaintable Landscape"
Cherry Tree: "Brutus's Feet"
Cold Mountain Review: "On Millet's *The Gleaners*"
Connecticut River Review: "Portrait of My Grandmother, Age Eight, Christmas Eve"
Copper Nickel: "National Poetry Month," "Practice Room"
The Cortland Review: "Forever Elegy"
Court Green: "Staring at Echenagusia's *Samson & Delilah* Every Morning for a Month"
Crannóg: "Marie-Thérèse Walter Mourns the Death of her Former Lover Pablo Picasso"
Crab Creek Review: "Zooming the Pledge"
Delmarva Review: "Grave By the Sea," "Heaven"
Diode: "Fifteen Wyeths"
The Dodge: "August Surfers at Assateague," "Sheep Above Vermilion Lakes"
Faultline: "Cut-Paper Work," "Echo"
The Freshwater Review: "The Unfinished Tomb"
Gargoyle: "Sleeping Quarters"
Hampden-Sydney Poetry Review: "A Wooden Rooster"
Innisfree Poetry Journal: "Before Photography"
Jet Fuel Review: "A Grecian Child's Commode," "May Night"
Los Angeles Review: "Consecration"
The Louisville Review: "Portrait / Self-Portrait"
Lucky Jefferson: "Child in Memphis"

The Maine Review: "Diagnosis"
The MacGuffin: "Ridge Church"
The National Poetry Review: "On an Unfinished Portrait of Thomas Hardy"
New Critique: "Figures on a Beach," "No. 6 (Violet, Green, and Red)," "On a Photograph of Archeologist Howard Carter, 1924"
North American Review: "Bosch Recalls the Brabant Fire"
Ocean State Review: "Exhibit," "The Lone Self-Portrait by Alberdt Klaver," "On a Photograph of Scott Weiland at the Virgin Festival, Calgary, 2008"
On the Seawall: "The Sutton Hoo Helmet"
Pacifica Literary Review: "Lesson Plan"
Pine Hills Review: "Selected Poems"
Pittsburgh Poetry Journal: "Window Cleaning"
Plume: "Red Abstraction," "Slaughterhouse Ruins at Aledo," "Watching Outtakes of Orson Wells Playing Othello on YouTube"
Potomac Review: "Franks Casket, Left Panel," "Fury Grove"
Quarter After Eight: "Harrison Park, Edinburgh, 1960"
Santa Fe Literary Review: "Fox Wake"
Sheepshead Review: "Apology for a Ghost"
The South Carolina Review: "The Fury of Paintbrushes"
Spoon River Poetry Review: "Quiz Bowl"
Sugar House Review: "Lecture with Slides"
Thrush: "On an Engraving of a Woman Entering an Abortion Clinic"
Wild Court: "A Dark Pool," "Somerset County Cold Case Photo, 1980"

"Practice Room" and "Word Problem" also featured on *Verse Daily*. "The Pillory and Steepled Dark" originally appeared in *America, We Call Your Name* (Sixteen Rivers Press, 2018).

I'm also grateful to William Hathaway, who first read these poems and whose insights proved invaluable. The greatest thanks are due to my family: Ann, James, Graham, and Roan.

CPSIA information can be obtained
at www.ICGtesting.com
Printed in the USA
JSHW020929170523
41820JS00003B/26